after work healthy

THE AUSTRALIAN Women's Weekly

CONTENTS

Australian cup and spoon measurements are metric. A conversion chart appears on page 78.

We all know how easy it is to be tempted by the convenience of takeaway food; it's fast, and isn't that what we want when we're in a hurry? Well, fast it may be, but it isn't very healthy. This book is full of fast recipes – many are on the table in around 30 minutes or less – and all are healthy, including the desserts. Fast and healthy – both very important issues when it comes to feeding today's busy families.

Pamela Clark

Food Director

SPICY BEEF AND BEAN SALAD

prep + cook time 30 minutes **serves** 4
nutritional count per serving 22.2g total fat (5.2g saturated fat); 2111kJ (505 cal); 30.9g carbohydrate; 40.4g protein; 9.3g fibre

35g packet taco seasoning mix
¼ cup (60ml) olive oil
600g piece beef eye fillet
2 tablespoons lime juice
1 clove garlic, crushed
420g can four-bean mix, rinsed, drained
310g can corn kernels, rinsed, drained
2 lebanese cucumbers (260g), chopped finely
1 small red onion (100g), chopped finely
1 large red capsicum (350g), chopped finely
½ cup coarsely chopped fresh coriander
1 fresh long red chilli, chopped finely

1 Combine seasoning, 1 tablespoon of the oil and beef in medium bowl. Cook beef on heated grill plate (or grill or barbecue) until cooked as desired. Cover; stand 5 minutes then slice thinly.
2 Meanwhile, whisk remaining oil, juice and garlic in large bowl. Add remaining ingredients; toss gently to combine. Serve beef with salad.

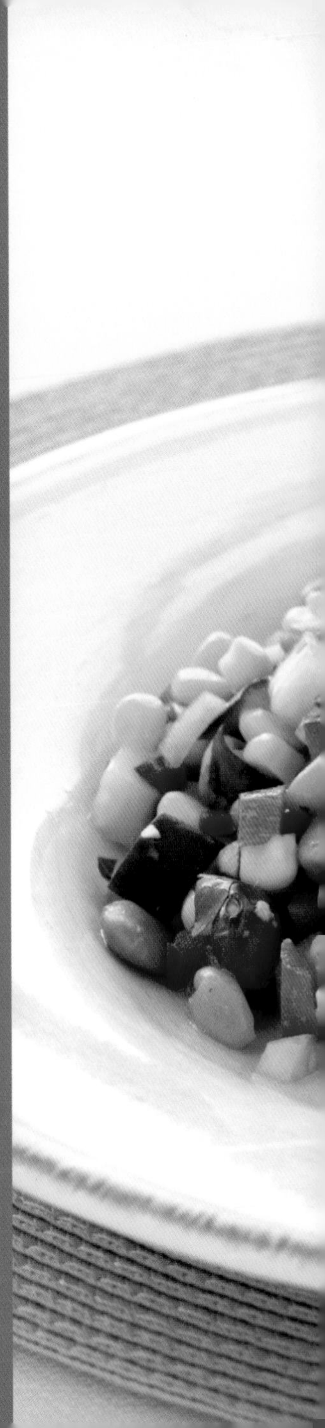

SALADS

chicken and cucumber salad

CHICKEN AND CUCUMBER SALAD

prep & cook time **25 minutes** serves **4**
nutritional count per serving **2g total fat (0.4g saturated fat); 706kJ (169 cal); 21.8g carbohydrate; 13.2g protein; 4.6g fibre**

150g chicken breast fillet, sliced thinly
1 clove garlic, crushed
1 tablespoon lemon juice
1 teaspoon finely chopped fresh oregano
¼ teaspoon sweet paprika
2 slices wholemeal lavash bread (120g)
cooking-oil spray
cucumber salad
1 telegraph cucumber (400g), halved lengthways, sliced thinly
1 large green capsicum (350g), sliced thinly
4 medium egg tomatoes (300g), seeded, sliced thinly
1 tablespoon coarsely chopped fresh dill
1 tablespoon coarsely chopped fresh oregano
¼ cup (60ml) white wine vinegar
2 teaspoons white sugar

1 Combine chicken, garlic, juice, oregano and paprika in medium bowl.
2 Meanwhile, preheat grill. Toast bread, both sides; break bread into large pieces.
3 Make cucumber salad.
4 Spray heated medium frying pan with cooking-oil spray; cook chicken in pan until cooked through.
5 Add chicken and bread to cucumber salad; toss gently. Serve immediately.
cucumber salad Combine ingredients in large bowl.

TURKISH LAMB AND YOGURT SALAD

prep & cook time **25 minutes** serves **4**
nutritional count per serving **10.8g total fat (3.4g saturated fat); 1062kJ (254 cal); 5.1g carbohydrate; 32.9g protein; 2.7g fibre**

600g lamb backstrap
2 tablespoons sumac
1 tablespoon olive oil
¼ cup (70g) yogurt
2 tablespoons lemon juice
250g cherry tomatoes, halved
2 lebanese cucumbers (260g), seeded, sliced thinly
½ cup loosely packed fresh flat-leaf parsley leaves
½ cup loosely packed fresh mint leaves
1 small red onion (100g), sliced thinly

1 Rub lamb with sumac. Heat oil in large frying pan; cook lamb, uncovered, until cooked as desired. Cover, stand 5 minutes then slice thinly.
2 Meanwhile, make dressing by whisking yogurt and juice in small jug.
3 Combine lamb and remaining ingredients in large bowl with dressing.

turkish lamb and yogurt salad

TURKEY, FIG AND SPINACH SALAD

prep time **10 minutes** serves **4**

Combine 2 tablespoons raspberry vinegar and 2 teaspoons walnut oil in screw-top jar; shake well. Quarter 6 large fresh figs and combine in large bowl with 100g baby spinach leaves, 100g coarsely chopped shaved turkey breast and the dressing.

TERIYAKI BEEF SALAD

prep & cook time **25 minutes** serves **4**

Combine ¼ cup teriyaki sauce and 2 teaspoons sesame oil in small jug. Combine half the teriyaki mixture with 500g piece beef rump steak in medium bowl. Cook beef on oiled grill plate. Cover, stand 10 minutes then slice beef thinly. Combine beef and remaining teriyaki mixture with 120g baby mesclun, 1 seeded, thinly sliced lebanese cucumber and 2 thinly sliced red radishes in large bowl.

FAST SALADS

SMOKED CHICKEN AND PEAR SALAD

prep time **15 minutes** serves **4**

Make red wine vinaigrette by combining ¼ cup red wine vinegar, 2 tablespoons balsamic vinegar and ¼ cup olive oil in screw-top jar; shake well. Combine 1 torn small radicchio, 1 torn small mignonette lettuce, 200g thinly sliced smoked chicken, 1 thinly sliced large pear, 1 thinly sliced medium red onion and vinaigrette in large bowl; toss gently.

ROCKET, PROSCIUTTO AND EGG SALAD

prep & cook time **30 minutes** serves **4**

Hard boil four eggs; cool slightly then peel and cut in half. Meanwhile, pan-fry 8 slices prosciutto until crisp; chop coarsely. Divide 120g baby rocket leaves and eggs among serving plates. Sprinkle with prosciutto and ¼ cup shaved parmesan cheese. Serve drizzled with ½ cup caesar dressing.

prawn and avocado salad with ginger dressing

PRAWN AND AVOCADO SALAD WITH GINGER DRESSING

prep time **25 minutes** serves **4**
nutritional count per serving **20.1g total fat (3.6g saturated fat); 1329kJ (318 cal); 5.2g carbohydrate; 29.1g protein; 3.5g fibre**

1kg cooked medium king prawns
200g snow peas, trimmed, sliced thinly
1 bunch fresh chives, cut into 4cm lengths
100g baby spinach leaves
1 medium avocado (250g), sliced thickly
ginger dressing
12cm piece fresh ginger (60g), grated
2 tablespoons olive oil
2 tablespoons lemon juice
1 teaspoon white sugar

1 Shell and devein prawns; cut in half lengthways.
2 Make ginger dressing.
3 Combine prawns in large bowl with snow peas, chives, spinach, avocado and dressing.
ginger dressing Press grated ginger between two spoons over screw-top jar; discard fibres. Add remaining ingredients; shake well.

PUMPKIN AND WHITE BEAN SALAD

prep & cook time **40 minutes** serves **4**
nutritional count per serving **4.4g total fat (0.9g saturated fat); 1091kJ (261 cal); 31.8g carbohydrate; 17.1g protein; 12.4g fibre**

1kg pumpkin, cut into 2cm pieces
2 x 400g cans cannellini beans, rinsed, drained
250g rocket, trimmed
1 cup loosely packed fresh coriander leaves
1 tablespoon sunflower seeds
preserved lemon dressing
¼ cup (60ml) lemon juice
2 teaspoons finely chopped fresh chives
2 teaspoons finely chopped preserved lemon rind
1 teaspoon olive oil
½ teaspoon white sugar

1 Preheat oven to 220°C/200°C fan-forced.
2 Place pumpkin, in single layer, on oven tray lined with baking paper; roast about 25 minutes or until tender.
3 Meanwhile, make preserved lemon dressing.
4 Combine beans, pumpkin and dressing in large bowl with rocket and coriander. Serve salad sprinkled with seeds.
preserved lemon dressing Combine ingredients in screw-top jar; shake well.

pumpkin and white bean salad

GRILLED CITRUS CHICKEN WITH ORANGE AND PISTACHIO COUSCOUS

prep + cook time 25 minutes **serves** 4
nutritional count per serving 18g total fat (4.4g saturated fat); 3620kJ (866 cal); 113g carbohydrate; 60.4g protein; 4.3g fibre

3 cloves garlic, crushed
1 tablespoon finely chopped fresh oregano
¼ cup (60ml) lemon juice
½ cup (170g) orange marmalade
2 fresh small red thai chillies, chopped finely
4 chicken breast fillets (800g)
2 cups (500ml) chicken stock
2 cups (400g) couscous
2 medium oranges (480g)
2 green onions, sliced thinly
⅓ cup (45g) roasted unsalted pistachios, chopped coarsely

1 Preheat oven to 200°C/180°C fan-forced. Oil and line oven tray.
2 Combine garlic, oregano, juice, marmalade and chilli in medium bowl; add chicken, turn to coat in mixture. Drain chicken, reserve marmalade mixture.
3 Cook chicken on heated oiled grill plate (or grill or barbecue) until browned both sides. Place chicken on oven tray, drizzle with reserved marmalade mixture; cook, uncovered, in oven, about 10 minutes or until chicken is cooked.
4 Meanwhile, bring stock to the boil in medium saucepan. Combine couscous with the stock in large heatproof bowl, cover; stand about 5 minutes or until liquid is absorbed, fluffing with fork occasionally. Segment oranges over couscous; stir in onion and nuts.
5 Serve couscous topped with chicken.

GRILLS

chicken, lemon and artichoke skewers

CHICKEN, LEMON AND ARTICHOKE SKEWERS

prep & cook time **35 minutes** serves **4**
nutritional count per serving **8.3g total fat (1.4g saturated fat); 1057kJ (252 cal); 7.9g carbohydrate; 34.3g protein; 8.2g fibre**

3 medium lemons (420g)
3 small red onions (300g)
500g chicken breast fillets, diced into 3cm pieces
400g can marinated quartered artichoke hearts, drained
300g button mushrooms
100g baby rocket leaves
2 tablespoons rinsed, drained baby capers
lemon dressing
1 tablespoon lemon juice
2 cloves garlic, crushed
½ teaspoon mild english mustard
1 tablespoon white wine vinegar
1 tablespoon olive oil

1 Make lemon dressing.
2 Cut each lemon into eight wedges; cut two of the onions into six wedges. Thread lemon and onion wedges, chicken, artichokes and mushrooms, alternately, onto skewers.
3 Place skewers in shallow dish; brush with half the dressing. Cook skewers on heated oiled grill plate (or grill or barbecue) until cooked through.
4 Meanwhile, slice remaining onion thinly, place in large bowl with rocket, capers and remaining dressing; toss gently. Divide salad among serving plates; top each with three skewers.
lemon dressing Combine ingredients in screw-top jar; shake well.
serve with **cooked brown rice.**

tip **If you have the time, soak 12 x 25cm-long bamboo skewers in cold water for 30 minutes to prevent them from scorching during cooking. Otherwise, wrap the ends in foil before placing on the barbecue or under the grill.**

balsamic rosemary grilled veal steaks

BALSAMIC ROSEMARY GRILLED VEAL STEAKS

prep + cook time **25 minutes** serves **4**
nutritional count per serving **11.3g total fat (1.8g saturated fat); 1016kJ (243 cal); 2.1g carbohydrate; 31.6g protein; 3.3g fibre**

2 tablespoons olive oil
2 tablespoons balsamic vinegar
1 tablespoon fresh rosemary leaves
2 cloves garlic, crushed
4 x 125g veal steaks
4 medium egg tomatoes (300g), halved
4 flat mushrooms (320g)

1 Combine oil, vinegar, rosemary, garlic and veal in medium bowl.
2 Cook veal on heated oiled grill plate (or grill or barbecue), brushing occasionally with vinegar mixture, until cooked as desired. Remove from heat; cover to keep warm.
3 Cook tomato and mushrooms on heated oiled grill plate until tender. Serve veal with tomato and mushrooms.

char-grilled steak and vegetables with baba ghanoush

CHAR-GRILLED STEAK AND VEGETABLES WITH BABA GHANOUSH

prep + cook time **35 minutes** serves **4**
nutritional count per serving **17.3g total fat (4.6g saturated fat); 1354kJ (324 cal); 5.9g carbohydrate; 34.2g protein; 3.6g fibre**

3 cloves garlic, crushed
2 tablespoons olive oil
2 teaspoons finely grated lemon rind
4 x 150g beef eye fillet steaks
2 medium red capsicums (400g), sliced thickly
2 large zucchini (300g), halved crossways, sliced thinly lengthways
½ cup (120g) baba ghanoush
⅓ cup loosely packed fresh mint leaves

1 Combine garlic, oil, rind, beef, capsicum and zucchini in large bowl. Cook beef and vegetables on heated grill plate (or grill or barbecue), in batches, until beef is cooked as desired and vegetables are tender.
2 Divide vegetables among serving plates; top with beef. Accompany with baba ghanoush and mint leaves.

CHILLI AND HONEY BARBECUED STEAK

prep + cook time **35 minutes** serves **4**
nutritional count per serving **15.2g total fat (5.4g saturated fat); 1605kJ (384 cal); 16.6g carbohydrate; 44g protein; 3.6g fibre**

2 tablespoons barbecue sauce
1 tablespoon worcestershire sauce
1 tablespoon honey
1 fresh long red chilli, chopped finely
1 clove garlic, crushed
4 x 220g beef new-york cut steaks

1 Combine sauces, honey, chilli and garlic in large bowl; add beef, turn to coat beef in honey mixture.
2 Cook beef on heated oiled grill plate (or grill or barbecue) until browned both sides and cooked as desired.
serve with **coleslaw.**

chilli and honey barbecued steak

TERIYAKI LAMB WITH CARROT SALAD

prep + cook time **35 minutes** serves **4**
nutritional count per serving **18.4g total fat (6.8g saturated fat); 1467kJ (351 cal); 7.7g carbohydrate; 35g protein; 3.7g fibre**

2 tablespoons japanese soy sauce
2 tablespoons mirin
1 teaspoon caster sugar
600g diced lamb
9 green onions

carrot salad

2 medium carrots (240g), cut into matchsticks
1 cup (80g) bean sprouts
1 small red onion (100g), sliced thinly
1 tablespoon toasted sesame seeds
2 teaspoons japanese soy sauce
1 tablespoon mirin
½ teaspoon white sugar
2 teaspoons peanut oil

1 Combine sauce, mirin, sugar and lamb in medium bowl.
2 Cut four 3cm-long pieces from trimmed root end of each onion.
3 Thread lamb and onion pieces, alternately, on skewers; cook on heated oiled grill plate (or grill or barbecue), brushing with soy mixture occasionally, until lamb is cooked as desired.
4 Meanwhile, make carrot salad. Serve teriyaki lamb with salad.

carrot salad Combine ingredients in medium bowl; toss gently.

tip **If you have the time, soak 12 x 25cm-long bamboo skewers in cold water for 30 minutes to prevent them from scorching during cooking. Otherwise, wrap the ends in foil before placing on the barbecue or under the grill.**

THAI CHICKEN BURGERS

prep & cook time **30 minutes** serves **4**

Combine 500g chicken mince, 1 egg and ¼ cup finely chopped thai basil leaves in medium bowl; shape into four patties. Cook patties in heated oiled large frying pan until cooked through. Cut 4 ciabatta rolls in half; toast cut sides. Sandwich patties, 40g baby asian greens and 2 tablespoons thai chilli jam between roll halves.

ROAST BEEF AND SLAW POCKETS

prep time **25 minutes** serves **4**

Combine 2 tablespoons olive oil, 2 teaspoons dijon mustard and 2 tablespoons each white wine vinegar and water in screw-top jar. Combine dressing with 2 cups finely shredded cabbage, 1 finely chopped small red onion, 1 finely grated small carrot and ¼ cup coarsely chopped fresh flat-leaf parsley in medium bowl. Split 4 pocket pitta breads a little more than halfway through; fill pockets with slaw and 200g sliced roast beef.

BURGERS, WRAPS & ROLLS

PAPRIKA LAMB WRAPS

prep & cook time **20 minutes** serves **4**

Sprinkle 600g lamb backstraps with 2 teaspoons sweet smoked paprika; cook on heated oiled grill plate (or grill or barbecue) until cooked. Cover lamb; stand 5 minutes then slice thinly. Meanwhile, warm 8 large (20cm) flour tortillas according to packet directions. Divide lamb, 80g baby rocket leaves, 1 cup drained semi-dried tomatoes in oil and ⅓ cup sour cream among tortillas; roll wraps to enclose filling.

ANTIPASTO CIABATTA ROLLS

prep & cook time **25 minutes** serves **4**

Thinly slice 1 medium eggplant; sprinkle slices with 1 tablespoon ground cumin. Cook eggplant, in batches, on heated oiled grill plate. Split and toast cut sides of 4 ciabatta bread rolls; spread rolls with ½ cup hummus, then sandwich eggplant, ⅔ cup drained sun-dried tomatoes and 40g baby rocket leaves among rolls.

lamb, bocconcini and gremolata stacks

LAMB, BOCCONCINI AND GREMOLATA STACKS

prep + cook time **25 minutes** serves **4**
nutritional count per serving **16.7g total fat (6.8g saturated fat); 1346kJ (322 cal); 3.4g carbohydrate; 38.8g protein; 1.2g fibre**

4 x 150g lamb leg steaks
1 tablespoon olive oil
1 large red capsicum (350g)
2 tablespoons lemon juice
100g bocconcini cheese, sliced thinly
gremolata
2 teaspoons finely grated lemon rind
2 cloves garlic, chopped finely
2 tablespoons finely chopped fresh basil

1 Make gremolata.
2 Using meat mallet, gently pound lamb between sheets of plastic wrap until 1cm thick. Cook lamb, in batches, on heated oiled grill plate (or grill or barbecue) until cooked as desired. Place lamb on oven tray.
3 Meanwhile, preheat grill. Quarter capsicum, discard seeds and membranes; place under grill, skin-side up, until skin blisters and blackens. Cover capsicum pieces in plastic or paper for 5 minutes; peel away skin then slice thickly. Combine capsicum and juice in small bowl.
4 Top steaks with capsicum then cheese; grill about 5 minutes or until cheese melts. Serve stacks sprinkled with gremolata.
gremolata Combine ingredients in small bowl.
serve with **baby rocket leaves.**

SPICED LAMB BURGER WITH TZATZIKI

prep + cook time **30 minutes** serves **4**
nutritional count per serving **21.1g total fat (7.5g saturated fat); 2604kJ (623 cal); 60g carbohydrate; 43.8g protein; 8g fibre**

500g lamb mince
½ small red onion (50g), chopped finely
1 egg yolk
½ cup (35g) stale breadcrumbs
2 tablespoons sumac
1 large loaf turkish bread (430g)
250g tzatziki
350g watercress, trimmed
¼ cup (60ml) lemon juice
225g can sliced beetroot, drained

1 Combine lamb, onion, egg yolk, breadcrumbs and half the sumac in medium bowl; shape mixture into four patties.
2 Cook patties on heated oiled grill plate (or grill or barbecue) until cooked through.
3 Meanwhile, preheat grill. Trim ends from bread; discard ends. Cut remaining bread into quarters then halve pieces horizontally. Toast, cut-sides up, under grill.
4 Combine remaining sumac and tzatziki in small bowl. Combine watercress and juice in another bowl.
5 Sandwich patties, tzatziki mixture, beetroot and watercress between toast slices.

note **Tzatziki is a Greek dip made with cucumber, yogurt, garlic and sometimes fresh mint. You can buy tzatziki ready-made in supermarkets and delis.**

spiced lamb burger with tzatziki

GINGER AND KAFFIR LIME FISH PARCELS

prep + cook time 20 minutes **serves** 4
nutritional count per serving 3.4g total fat (0.5g saturated fat); 648kJ (155 cal); 6.3g carbohydrate; 30.4g protein; 0.2g fibre

4 x 180g ocean perch fillets
3 green onions, sliced thinly
5cm piece fresh ginger (25g), sliced thinly
4 fresh kaffir lime leaves, shredded finely
2 teaspoons sesame oil

1 Preheat oven to 180°C/160°C fan-forced.
2 Place each fillet on large square of baking paper or oiled foil; top each with onion, ginger and lime leaves, drizzle with oil. Gather corners together; fold to enclose, tie with kitchen string if necessary.
3 Place parcels on oven trays; cook about 15 minutes or until fish is cooked through.
4 Remove fish from parcel, discard topping from fish.
serve with steamed jasmine rice; accompany with lime wedges.

note We used perch in this recipe, but you can use any firm white fish fillet you like – blue eye, bream, swordfish, ling or whiting are all good choices. Check for any small pieces of bone in the fillets and use tweezers to remove them.

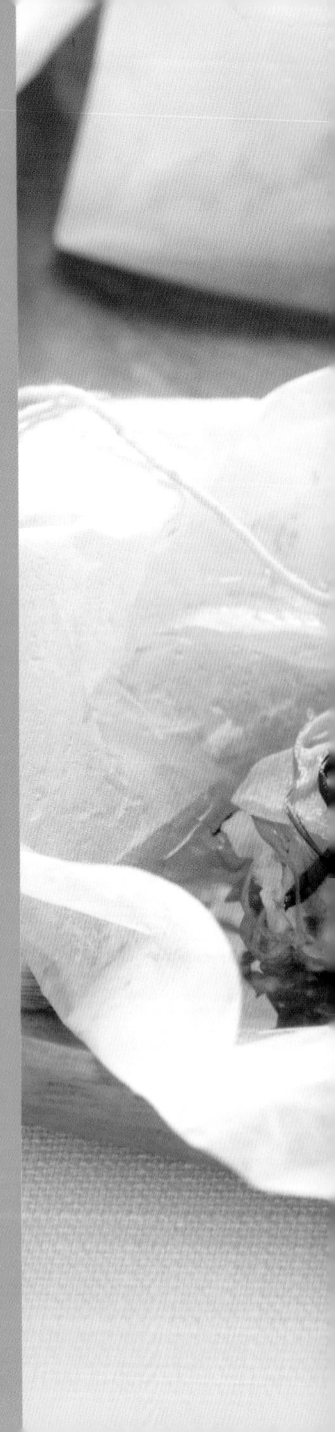

ROASTS & BAKES

meatloaves with thai flavours

MEATLOAVES WITH THAI FLAVOURS

prep & cook time **40 minutes** serves **4**
nutritional count per serving **16.4g total fat (7.9g saturated fat); 1496kJ (358 cal); 16.1g carbohydrate; 35.4g protein; 1.7g fibre**

600g pork mince
⅓ cup (80ml) oyster sauce
2 cloves garlic, crushed
1 egg
1 fresh small red thai chilli, chopped finely
½ cup (50g) packaged breadcrumbs
½ cup (125ml) coconut milk
⅓ cup finely chopped thai basil
250g gai lan, cut into 10cm lengths

1 Preheat oven to 240°C/220°C fan-forced.
2 Combine mince, 2 tablespoons of the sauce, garlic, egg, chilli, breadcrumbs, coconut milk and basil in large bowl; shape into four rectangular meatloaves. Wrap each meatloaf in oiled foil; place in large shallow baking dish. Cook meatloaves 10 minutes.
3 Remove foil; brush meatloaves with another tablespoon of the sauce. Cook about 10 minutes, turning occasionally, or until cooked through.
4 Meanwhile, boil, steam or microwave gai lan until tender; combine with remaining sauce in large bowl. Serve gai lan topped with sliced meatloaves.
serve with **steamed jasamine rice.**

BALSAMIC CHICKEN WITH EGGPLANT PUREE

prep & cook time **35 minutes** serves **4**
nutritional count per serving **21.4g total fat (6.3g saturated fat); 1643kJ (393 cal); 12.2g carbohydrate; 36g protein; 4.5g fibre**

8 chicken drumsticks (1.2kg)
2 tablespoons balsamic vinegar
2 tablespoons brown sugar
1 large eggplant (500g), halved lengthways
6 medium egg tomatoes (450g), halved
⅓ cup loosely packed fresh baby basil leaves

1 Preheat oven to 240°C/220°C fan-forced.
2 Combine chicken, vinegar and sugar in large shallow baking dish. Cover dish; roast chicken 15 minutes.
3 Meanwhile, pierce eggplant all over with fork; place, cut-side down, on oiled oven tray. Roast, uncovered, about 15 minutes or until tender. When cool enough to handle, peel eggplant; discard skin. Blend or process eggplant flesh until smooth.
4 Uncover chicken; add tomato to dish. Roast, uncovered, about 15 minutes or until chicken is cooked through.
5 Serve chicken with eggplant puree and tomato; drizzle with pan juices then sprinkle with basil.
serve with **a salad of mixed green leaves.**

balsamic chicken with eggplant puree

lime and chilli roasted snapper

LIME AND CHILLI ROASTED SNAPPER

prep & cook time **30 minutes** serves **4**
nutritional count per serving **15.1g total fat (3.5g saturated fat); 1354kJ (324 cal); 55g carbohydrate; 40.6g protein; 1.8g fibre**

4 x 500g plate-size snapper, cleaned
2cm piece fresh ginger (10g), sliced thinly
2 cloves garlic, sliced thinly
8 fresh kaffir lime leaves
1 fresh long red chilli, sliced thinly
2 tablespoons peanut oil
1 cup loosely packed fresh coriander leaves
chilli lime dressing
⅓ cup (80ml) sweet chilli sauce
¼ cup (60ml) fish sauce
¼ cup (60 2 teaspoons peanut oil

1 Preheat oven to 240°C/220°C fan-forced.
2 Rinse fish inside and out under cold running water; pat dry with absorbent paper.
3 Divide ginger, garlic, lime leaves and chilli among fish cavities; rub fish all over with oil.
4 Place fish in two shallow oiled baking dishes; roast, uncovered, about 15 minutes or until cooked through.
5 Meanwhile, make chilli lime dressing.
6 Drizzle fish with dressing, sprinkle with coriander leaves.
chilli lime dressing Combine ingredients in screw-top jar; shake well.
serve with **steamed asian greens.**

ROASTED PORK FILLET WITH PEAR AND APRICOT RELISH

prep & cook time **30 minutes** serves **4**
nutritional count per serving **8g total fat (1.8g saturated fat); 1400kJ (335 cal); 29.2g carbohydrate; 34.2g protein; 3.3g fibre**

410g can sliced pears in natural juice
410g can apricot halves in natural juice
600g pork fillets
1 tablespoon olive oil
½ cup (125ml) water
2 tablespoons white vinegar
1 fresh long red chilli, chopped finely

roasted pork fillet with pear and apricot relish

¼ cup (40g) sultanas
2 tablespoons white sugar

1 Preheat oven to 240°C/220°C fan-forced.
2 Drain pears over small bowl. Reserve juice; chop pears coarsely. Drain apricots, discarding juice. Chop apricots coarsely.
3 Place pork in oiled baking dish; drizzle with oil. Roast, uncovered, about 20 minutes or until cooked as desired. Cover; stand 5 minutes then slice thickly.
4 Meanwhile, combine pear, apricot, reserved juice and remaining ingredients in medium saucepan; bring to the boil. Reduce heat; simmer, uncovered, about 20 minutes or until relish thickens slightly. Serve pork with relish.
serve with **steamed snow peas.**

CHILLI LAMB NOODLES WITH BUK CHOY

prep & cook time 35 minutes **serves** 4
nutritional count per serving 14.4g total fat (4.7g saturated fat); 1877kJ (449 cal); 44.5g carbohydrate; 34.3g protein; 5.3g fibre

400g fresh thin rice noodles
1 tablespoon peanut oil
500g lamb mince
3 cloves garlic, crushed
2 fresh small red thai chillies, chopped finely
400g buk choy, sliced thinly
2 tablespoons tamari
1 tablespoon fish sauce
2 tablespoons kecap manis
4 green onions, sliced thinly
1 cup firmly packed thai basil leaves
3 cups (240g) bean sprouts

1 Place noodles in medium heatproof bowl; cover with boiling water, separate with fork, drain.
2 Heat oil in wok; stir-fry mince until browned. Add garlic and chilli; stir-fry until fragrant. Add noodles, buk choy and sauces; stir-fry until buk choy just wilts.
3 Remove from heat; stir in onion, basil and sprouts. Top with sliced chilli to serve.

note Tamari is a thick, dark sauce soy sauce; it has a distinctive mellow flavour and is used mainly as a dipping sauce or for basting. Tamari is available from most supermarkets and Asian food stores.

STIR-FRIES

pork kway teow

PORK KWAY TEOW

prep + cook time **30 minutes** serves **4**
nutritional count per serving **15.6g total fat (4.7g saturated fat); 1660kJ (397 cal); 29g carbohydrate; 33.9g protein; 1.5g fibre**

400g fresh wide rice noodles
1 tablespoon peanut oil
600g pork mince
1 medium brown onion (150g), sliced thinly
1 medium red capsicum (200g), sliced thinly
10cm stick fresh lemon grass (20g), chopped finely
2 tablespoons light soy sauce
¼ cup (60ml) lemon juice
1 tablespoon grated palm sugar
2 fresh small red thai chillies, chopped finely
1 cup coarsely chopped fresh coriander

1 Place noodles in large heatproof bowl, cover with boiling water; separate noodles with fork, drain.
2 Heat half the oil in wok; stir-fry pork until cooked through. Remove from wok.
3 Heat remaining oil in same wok; stir-fry onion, capsicum and lemon grass until onion softens.
4 Return pork to wok with noodles and combined sauce, juice and sugar; stir-fry until heated through. Remove from heat: stir through chilli and coriander.

STIR-FRIED PORK WITH BUK CHOY AND RICE NOODLES

prep + cook time **20 minutes** serves **4**
nutritional count per serving **6.7g total fat (1.6g saturated fat); 1492kJ (357 cal); 31.6g carbohydrate; 37.9g protein; 2.9g fibre**

¼ cup (60ml) oyster sauce
2 tablespoons light soy sauce
2 tablespoons sweet sherry
1 tablespoon brown sugar
1 clove garlic, crushed
1 star anise, crushed
pinch five-spice powder
400g fresh rice noodles
2 teaspoons sesame oil
600g pork fillets, sliced thinly
700g baby buk choy, chopped coarsely

stir-fried pork with buk choy and rice noodles

1 Combine sauces, sherry, sugar, garlic, star anise and five-spice in small jug.
2 Place noodles in large heatproof bowl, cover with boiling water; separate noodles with fork, drain.
3 Heat oil in wok; stir-fry pork, in batches, until cooked as desired. Return pork to wok with sauce mixture, noodles and buk choy; stir-fry until buk choy is wilted.

lamb teriyaki with broccolini

LAMB TERIYAKI WITH BROCCOLINI

prep & cook time **25 minutes** serves **4**
nutritional count per serving **15.9g total fat (4.3g saturated fat); 1626kJ (389 cal); 14.1g carbohydrate; 45.7g protein; 3.4g fibre**

1 tablespoon vegetable oil
800g lamb strips
4 green onions, chopped coarsely
3cm piece fresh ginger (15g), grated
175g broccolini, chopped coarsely
150g green beans, trimmed, halved crossways
⅓ cup (80ml) teriyaki sauce
2 tablespoons honey
2 teaspoons sesame oil
1 tablespoon roasted sesame seeds

1 Heat half the vegetable oil in wok; stir-fry lamb, in batches, until browned.
2 Heat remaining vegetable oil in wok; stir-fry onion and ginger until onion softens. Add broccolini and beans; stir-fry until vegetables are tender. Remove from wok.
3 Add sauce, honey and sesame oil to wok; bring to the boil. Boil, uncovered, about 3 minutes or until sauce thickens slightly. Return lamb and vegetables to wok; stir-fry until hot. Sprinkle with seeds.

CHILLI ORANGE PORK

prep & cook time **20 minutes** serves **4**
nutritional count per serving **2.9g total fat (0.7g saturated fat); 694kJ (166 cal); 10.9g carbohydrate; 19.2g protein; 4.4g fibre**

1 teaspoon peanut oil
250g pork fillet, sliced thinly
1 medium red onion (170g), sliced thinly
2 cloves garlic, sliced thinly
1 fresh long red chilli, sliced thinly
½ teaspoon chilli flakes
150g sugar snap peas, trimmed
150g snow peas, trimmed
1 cup (120g) frozen peas
2 tablespoons water
¼ cup (60ml) light soy sauce
2 tablespoons sweet sherry
1 teaspoon finely grated orange rind
2 tablespoons orange juice
4 green onions, sliced thickly

1 Heat oil in wok; stir-fry pork until browned. Remove from wok.
2 Add red onion, garlic, sliced chilli and chilli flakes; stir-fry until fragrant. Add peas and the water; stir-fry until peas are tender.
3 Return pork to wok with sauce, sherry, rind, juice and green onion; stir-fry until hot.

chilli orange pork

chilli fried rice with chicken and broccolini

CHILLI FRIED RICE WITH CHICKEN AND BROCCOLINI

prep & cook time **25 minutes** serves **4**
nutritional count per serving **15.3g total fat (3.8g saturated fat); 1881kJ (450 cal); 44.6g carbohydrate; 30.9g protein; 4.1g fibre**

1 tablespoon peanut oil
3 eggs, beaten lightly
1 medium brown onion (150g), sliced thinly
1 clove garlic, crushed
2 fresh long red chillies, sliced thinly
175g broccolini, chopped coarsely
2 cups (320g) shredded barbecued chicken
3 cups cooked white long-grain rice
1 tablespoon light soy sauce
1 tablespoon hoisin sauce

1 Heat about a third of the oil in wok; add half the egg, swirl wok to make a thin omelette. Remove omelette from wok; roll then cut into thin strips. Repeat process using another third of the oil and remaining egg.
2 Heat remaining oil in wok; stir-fry onion, garlic and chilli until onion softens. Add broccolini; stir-fry until tender.
3 Add remaining ingredients to wok; stir-fry until hot. Add omelette; toss gently.

notes **Cook 1 cup (200g) white long-grain rice the night before making this recipe; refrigerate it, spread thinly on a tray, covered, overnight. You need a large barbecued chicken, weighing approximately 900g, for this recipe.**

FIVE-SPICE BEEF AND ASIAN GREENS

prep & cook time **20 minutes** serves **4**
nutritional count per serving **3.4g total fat (0.9g saturated fat); 640kJ (153 cal); 16.1g carbohydrate; 12.4g protein; 3.6g fibre**

150g beef fillet, sliced thinly
2cm piece fresh ginger (10g), grated
1 teaspoon five-spice powder
1 teaspoon peanut oil
¼ cup (60ml) dark soy sauce
2 tablespoons water
2 tablespoons honey
2 teaspoons lemon juice

five-spice beef and asian greens

500g gai lan, trimmed, quartered crossways
350g choy sum, trimmed, quartered crossways
150g sugar snap peas, trimmed
½ teaspoon sesame seeds

1 Combine beef, ginger and five-spice in small bowl.
2 Heat oil in wok; stir-fry beef until browned. Remove beef from pan.
3 Add sauce, the water, honey and juice to wok; bring to the boil. Simmer, 2 minutes.
4 Return beef to wok with vegetables; stir-fry until gai lan is tender. Serve sprinkled with seeds.

chilli, salt and pepper seafood

CHILLI, SALT AND PEPPER SEAFOOD

prep & cook time **30 minutes** serves **4**
nutritional count per serving **11g total fat (2.2g saturated fat); 1070kJ (256 cal); 2.7g carbohydrate; 35.8g protein; 1.2g fibre**

500g uncooked medium king prawns
300g cleaned squid hoods
300g scallops, roe removed
2 teaspoons sea salt
½ teaspoon cracked black pepper
½ teaspoon five-spice powder
2 fresh small red thai chillies, chopped finely
2 tablespoons peanut oil
150g sugar snap peas, trimmed
2 tablespoons light soy sauce
1 lime, cut into wedges

1 Shell and devein prawns, leaving tails intact. Cut squid down centre to open out; score inside in diagonal pattern then cut into thick strips.
2 Combine seafood, salt, pepper, five-spice and chilli in large bowl.
3 Heat half the oil in wok; stir-fry seafood, in batches, until cooked. Heat remaining oil in wok; stir-fry peas until tender. Return seafood to wok with sauce; stir-fry until hot. Serve with wedges.

HONEY PRAWNS WITH PINEAPPLE

prep & cook time **30 minutes** serves **4**
nutritional count per serving **2g total fat (0.3g saturated fat); 807kJ (193 cal); 16.7g carbohydrate; 24.3g protein; 4g fibre**

800g uncooked medium king prawns
1 teaspoon peanut oil
1 large red capsicum (350g), chopped coarsely
150g snow peas, trimmed
2 cloves garlic, crushed
½ small pineapple (450g), chopped coarsely
230g can bamboo shoots, rinsed, drained
2 tablespoons tamarind concentrate
2 tablespoons kecap manis
1 tablespoon honey

1 Shell and devein prawns, leaving tails intact.
2 Heat oil in wok; stir-fry prawns, capsicum, peas and garlic until prawns are changed in colour. Add remaining ingredients; stir-fry until hot.
serve with **steamed jasmine rice.**

note **Tamarind concentrate is the commercial distillation of tamarind pulp into a condensed paste. Use straight from the container, with no soaking or straining required, or dilute with water according to taste. Found in supermarkets and Asian food stores.**

honey prawns with pineapple

CHICKEN AND PASTA NAPOLETANA

prep + cook time 35 minutes **serves** 4
nutritional count per serving 20.5g total fat (5.8g saturated fat); 2546kJ (609 cal); 66.3g carbohydrate; 35.9g protein; 5.1g fibre

250g cherry tomatoes
1 tablespoon olive oil
375g fettuccine pasta
2 cups (320g) shredded barbecued chicken
⅔ cup (50g) shaved parmesan cheese
50g baby spinach leaves
⅔ cup firmly packed fresh basil leaves
⅓ cup (80ml) lemon juice
1 tablespoon olive oil
2 cloves garlic, crushed

1 Preheat oven to 240°C/220°C fan-forced.
2 Combine tomatoes and oil in medium shallow baking dish; roast, uncovered, about 10 minutes or until tomatoes are softened.
3 Meanwhile, cook pasta in large saucepan of boiling water, uncovered, until just tender; drain.
4 Place tomato mixture and pasta in large bowl with chicken, cheese, spinach and basil; pour over combined juice, oil and garlic, toss gently.

note You need half a large barbecued chicken (approximately 500g) to get the amount of shredded meat required for this recipe.

PASTA

lamb and pasta niçoise

LAMB AND PASTA NIÇOISE

prep & cook time **30 minutes** serves **4**
nutritional count per serving **19.5g total fat (6.9g saturated fat); 2838kJ (679 cal); 75.5g carbohydrate; 45.4g protein; 8.2g fibre**

375g penne pasta
1 tablespoon olive oil
600g lamb fillets
4 large tomatoes (880g), chopped coarsely
2 cloves garlic, crushed
1 fresh long red chilli, chopped finely
1 cup (120g) seeded black olives, chopped coarsely
2 tablespoons rinsed drained baby capers
12 (150g) drained marinated artichoke hearts, quartered
1 cup loosely packed fresh flat-leaf parsley leaves

1 Cook pasta in large saucepan of boiling water, uncovered, until just tender; drain.
2 Meanwhile, heat half the oil in large frying pan; cook lamb, in batches, until browned all over and cooked as desired. Cover; stand 5 minutes then slice thinly.
3 Heat remaining oil in large saucepan; cook tomato, garlic and chilli, stirring, until tomato softens. Stir in olives, capers and artichoke.
4 Return lamb to pan with pasta and parsley; toss gently until heated through.

tuna and chilli pasta

TUNA AND CHILLI PASTA

prep & cook time **15 minutes** serves **4**
nutritional count per serving **22.3g total fat (3.2g saturated fat); 2617kJ (626 cal); 67.5g carbohydrate; 32.5g protein; 4.8g fibre**

375g angel hair pasta
425g can tuna in oil
4 cloves garlic, sliced thinly
1 teaspoon dried chilli flakes
⅓ cup (80ml) dry white wine
400g can chopped tomatoes
1 tablespoon lemon juice

1 Cook pasta in large saucepan of boiling water until tender; drain, reserving ¼ cup cooking liquid. Rinse pasta under cold water, drain.
2 Meanwhile, drain tuna, reserving 2 tablespoons of the oil. Heat oil in medium frying pan, add garlic; cook, stirring, until fragrant. Add chilli and wine; cook, stirring, until wine is almost evaporated. Add undrained tomatoes, tuna and reserved cooking liquid; simmer until liquid has reduced slightly. Remove from heat; stir in juice. Combine pasta and sauce in large bowl.
serve with **coarsely chopped fresh basil leaves.**

pasta with capers and anchovies

PASTA WITH CAPERS AND ANCHOVIES

prep + cook time **20 minutes** serves **4**
nutritional count per serving **11.1g total fat (1.7g saturated fat); 1781kJ (426 cal); 65.6g carbohydrate; 13.3g protein; 3.8g fibre**

375g spaghetti
2 tablespoons olive oil
3 cloves garlic, sliced thinly
¼ cup (50g) rinsed, drained baby capers
10 drained anchovy fillets, chopped finely
1 tablespoon finely grated lemon rind
1 tablespoon lemon juice

1 Cook pasta in large saucepan of boiling water until tender; drain.
2 Meanwhile, heat oil in medium frying pan; cook garlic, stirring, until fragrant. Add capers and anchovies; stir gently until hot. Pour garlic mixture over pasta; stir in rind and juice.

tip **Stir in ¼ cup coarsely chopped fresh flat-leaf parsley or a handful of baby rocket leaves before serving. A teaspoon of dried chilli flakes added to the cooked garlic will give a little extra bite.**

LINGUINE MARINARA

prep & cook time **20 minutes** serves **2**
nutritional count per serving **7.2g total fat (1.8g saturated fat); 2387kJ (571 cal); 61.9g carbohydrate; 60.1g protein; 6.4g fibre**

150g linguine pasta
400g marinara mix
1 small brown onion (80g), chopped finely
2 cloves garlic, crushed
1 fresh small red thai chilli, chopped finely
400g can diced tomatoes
⅓ cup coarsely chopped fresh flat-leaf parsley

1 Cook pasta in large saucepan of boiling water until tender; drain.
2 Meanwhile, cook marinara mix in heated large frying pan, stirring, 2 minutes; drain.
3 Add onion, garlic and chilli to same heated pan; cook, stirring, about 5 minutes or until onion softens. Add undrained tomatoes; cook, stirring, 5 minutes. Return seafood to pan; cook, stirring occasionally, about 2 minutes. Stir in parsley.
4 Serve pasta with marinara sauce.

note **Marinara mix is a mixture of uncooked, chopped seafood available from fish markets and fishmongers. Don't overcook the seafood; if you do, it will be tough and leathery.**

linguine marinara

lemon, pea and ricotta pasta

LEMON, PEA AND RICOTTA PASTA

prep + cook time **15 minutes** serves **4**
nutritional count per serving **15.6g total fat (4.7g saturated fat); 2123kJ (508 cal); 69g carbohydrate; 19g protein; 6.9g fibre**

375g angel hair pasta
2 cups (240g) frozen peas
2 tablespoons olive oil
2 cloves garlic, sliced thinly
2 teaspoons finely grated lemon rind
½ cup (125ml) lemon juice
¾ cup (180g) ricotta cheese, crumbled

1 Cook pasta in large saucepan of boiling water until tender; add peas during last minute of pasta cooking time. Drain, reserving ¼ cup cooking liquid. Rinse pasta and peas under cold water; drain.
2 Meanwhile, heat oil in small frying pan; cook garlic, stirring, until fragrant.
3 Combine pasta and peas in large bowl with reserved cooking liquid, garlic mixture, rind and juice; stir in cheese.

tip **Stir in ⅓ cup loosely packed fresh mint leaves. Fetta can be used in place of the ricotta.**

SPAGHETTI BOLOGNESE

prep & cook time **35 minutes** serves **4**
nutritional count per serving **15.4g total fat (5g saturated fat); 2834kJ (678 cal); 79.1g carbohydrate; 44.4g protein; 10.7g fibre**

1 tablespoon olive oil
1 medium brown onion (150g), chopped coarsely
2 cloves garlic, crushed
2 medium carrots (240g), chopped coarsely
2 stalks celery (300g), trimmed, chopped coarsely
500g beef mince
2 x 400g cans crushed tomatoes
½ cup (125ml) dry red wine
⅓ cup (95g) tomato paste
1 teaspoon white sugar
200g button mushrooms, sliced thinly
¼ cup finely chopped fresh basil

spaghetti bolognese

375g spaghetti
¼ cup (20g) finely grated parmesan cheese

1 Heat oil in large saucepan; cook onion, garlic, carrot and celery, stirring, until vegetables soften.
2 Add mince to pan; cook, stirring, until mince changes colour. Add undrained tomatoes, wine, paste and sugar; cook, stirring occasionally, about 15 minutes or until sauce thickens slightly. Add mushrooms and basil; reduce heat, simmer, uncovered, 10 minutes.
3 Meanwhile, cook pasta in large saucepan of boiling water, uncovered, until just tender; drain.
4 Divide pasta among serving bowls; top with bolognese sauce, sprinkle with cheese.
serve with **ciabatta bread and a green salad.**

warm pasta provençale

WARM PASTA PROVENÇALE

prep & cook time **30 minutes** serves **6**
nutritional count per serving **16.9g total fat (3.4g saturated fat); 2203kJ (527 cal); 57.4g carbohydrate; 32g protein; 7.5g fibre**

375g rigatoni pasta
600g lamb fillets
¾ cup (115g) seeded black kalamata olives, halved
1 cup (150g) drained semi-dried tomatoes in oil, chopped coarsely
400g can artichoke hearts, drained, halved
1 small red onion (100g), sliced thinly
60g baby rocket leaves
½ cup (120g) green olive tapenade
2 tablespoons olive oil
2 tablespoons lemon juice

1 Cook pasta in large saucepan of boiling water until tender.
2 Meanwhile, cook lamb, uncovered, in heated oiled large frying pan until cooked as desired. Cover; stand 5 minutes then slice thickly.
3 Combine drained pasta with lamb and remaining ingredients in large bowl. Serve warm.

SUMMER SPAGHETTI WITH PEA PESTO AND HAM

prep & cook time **25 minutes** serves **6**
nutritional count per serving **15.3g total fat (3.1g saturated fat); 2006kJ (480 cal); 60.9g carbohydrate; 21.2g protein; 5.9g fibre**

500g spaghetti
2 cups (240g) frozen peas
2 cloves garlic
¼ cup (40g) roasted pine nuts
½ cup loosely packed fresh basil leaves
⅓ cup loosely packed fresh mint leaves
½ cup (40g) flaked parmesan cheese
2 tablespoons olive oil
200g finely sliced leg ham
⅓ cup (80ml) lemon juice

1 Cook pasta in large saucepan of boiling water until just tender; drain.
2 Meanwhile, microwave peas on HIGH (100%) about 2 minutes or until tender; drain. Blend or process peas with garlic, nuts, herbs, cheese and oil until mixture forms a thick puree.
3 Combine pea pesto, ham and juice with pasta in large bowl.
serve with **extra parmesan cheese.**

summer spaghetti with pea pesto and ham

HAM, TOMATO AND ROCKET PIZZA

prep & cook time **20 minutes** serves **4**

Preheat oven to 200°C/180°C fan-forced. Place 4 large wholemeal pitta bread on oven trays; spread 1 tablespoon tomato paste over each bread. Divide 300g shaved ham, 500g halved cherry tomatoes and ½ thinly sliced small red onion between bread; dollop ⅔ cup low-fat ricotta cheese between pizzas. Bake about 10 minutes. Serve sprinkled with 60g baby rocket leaves and ⅓ cup finely shredded fresh basil.

RICOTTA, BASIL AND PINE NUT PIZZA

prep & cook time **20 minutes** serves **4**

Preheat oven to 220°C/200°C fan-forced. Place 4 large pitta breads on oven trays; spread with 1 cup bottled tomato pasta sauce. Divide 1 cup ricotta cheese and ¼ cup roasted pine nuts among pittas; cook, uncovered, about 10 minutes or until pitta bases are crisp and topping is heated through. Serve topped with 1 cup loosely packed fresh basil leaves and 50g baby spinach leaves.

PIZZA

PIZZA CAPRESE

prep & cook time **20 minutes** serves **4**

Preheat oven to 220°C/200°C fan-forced. Oil two oven trays. Combine 1 tablespoon olive oil, 2 crushed garlic cloves and 2 tablespoons finely chopped fresh sage leaves in small bowl; spread over 2 x 335g pizza bases then top with 100g thinly sliced ham and 200g thinly sliced fontina cheese. Cook, uncovered, about 10 minutes.

note **We used large (25cm diameter) packaged pizza bases for this recipe. Fontina is an Italian cows-milk cheese that has a smooth but firm texture and a mild, nutty flavour. Mozzarella can be substituted for the fontina.**

PRAWN AND GRILLED CAPSICUM PIZZA

prep & cook time **30 minutes** serves **4**

Preheat oven to 220°C/200°C fan-forced. Oil two oven trays. Shell and devein 720g uncooked medium king prawns. Combine 1 tablespoon olive oil, 4 crushed garlic cloves and 2 finely chopped fresh small red thai chillies in large bowl with prawns. Cook prawn mixture in heated large frying pan until prawns are changed in colour. Spread 4 x 112g pizza bases with ⅓ cup tomato paste; top with ½ cup coarsely grated mozzarella cheese, prawns and a drained 270g jar coarsely chopped char-grilled capsicum in oil. Cook, uncovered, about 15 minutes. Sprinkle pizzas with ¼ cup flaked parmesan cheese and ⅓ cup loosely packed fresh basil leaves.

CHICKEN WITH PECAN HONEY SAUCE

prep & cook time 35 minutes **serves** 4
nutritional count per serving 7.2g total fat (1.3g saturated fat); 560kJ (134 cal); 5.1g carbohydrate; 10.6g protein; 1g fibre

2 tablespoons olive oil
4 x 200g breast fillets
3 shallots (75g), chopped finely
1 clove garlic, crushed
½ cup (125ml) dry white wine
½ cup (125ml) chicken stock
2 tablespoons honey
2 teaspoons dijon mustard
½ cup (60g) roasted pecans, chopped coarsely
100g mesclun
1 tablespoon lemon juice
2 small pears (360g), sliced thinly

1 Heat half the oil in large frying pan; cook chicken, uncovered, until cooked through. Remove from pan; cover to keep warm.
2 Cook shallot and garlic in same heated pan, stirring, until onion softens. Add wine; bring to the boil. Reduce heat; simmer, uncovered, until liquid is reduced by half. Add stock, honey and mustard; cook, stirring, about 5 minutes or until liquid is reduced by half. Remove from heat; stir in nuts.
3 Place mesclun with combined juice and remaining oil in medium bowl; toss gently. Cut chicken in half crossways; drizzle with sauce. Serve chicken with mesclun and pear.

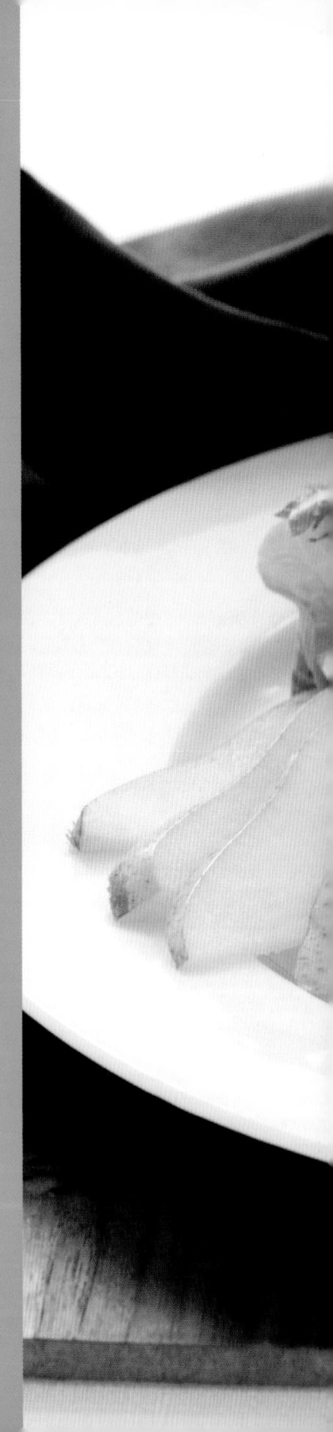

POT & PAN

fish with chunky tomato, anchovy and caper sauce

FISH WITH CHUNKY TOMATO, ANCHOVY AND CAPER SAUCE

prep + cook time **30 minutes** serves **4**
nutritional count per serving **7.1g total fat (1.1g saturated fat); 1099kJ (263 cal); 6.4g carbohydrate; 41.8g protein; 2.8g fibre**

1 tablespoon olive oil
4 x 200g blue-eye fillets
1 medium brown onion (150g), chopped finely
2 cloves garlic, crushed
4 medium tomatoes (600g), peeled, seeded, chopped coarsely
4 drained anchovy fillets, chopped finely
1 tablespoon rinsed drained capers
1 teaspoon white sugar
¼ cup coarsely chopped fresh flat-leaf parsley

1 Heat half the oil in large frying pan; cook fish, uncovered, until cooked as desired.
2 Meanwhile, heat remaining oil in small saucepan; cook onion and garlic, stirring, until onion softens. Add tomato; cook, stirring, 1 minute. Remove from heat; stir in anchovy, capers, sugar and parsley. Serve fish with sauce.
serve with **a leafy green salad and accompany with lemon wedges.**

note **We used blue eye in this recipe, but you can use any firm white fish fillet you like – swordfish, ling, bream, whiting or sea perch are all good choices.**

STEAMED SALMON WITH BURNT ORANGE SAUCE

prep + cook time **35 minutes** serves **4**
nutritional count per serving **19.1g total fat (3.8g saturated fat); 1940kJ (464 cal); 29.4g carbohydrate; 41.6g protein; 3.4g fibre**

½ cup (110g) caster sugar
⅓ cup (80ml) water
1 teaspoon finely grated orange rind
¼ cup (60ml) orange juice
1 tablespoon olive oil
1 tablespoon chinese cooking wine
4 x 200g salmon fillets
350g watercress, trimmed

1 Combine sugar and the water in small saucepan; stir, without boiling, until sugar dissolves, bring to the boil. Reduce heat; simmer, uncovered, without stirring, until mixture is a light caramel colour.
2 Remove pan from heat; allow bubbles to subside. Carefully stir in rind and juice; return pan to low heat. Stir until any pieces of caramel melt. Remove pan from heat; stir in oil and cooking wine.
3 Meanwhile, place fish in large bamboo steamer set over large saucepan of simmering water; steam, covered, 15 minutes. Serve fish with watercress; drizzle with sauce.

steamed salmon with burnt orange sauce

CHICKPEA RATATOUILLE

prep + cook time **35 minutes** serves **4**
nutritional count per serving **10.8g total fat (1.4g saturated fat); 857kJ (205 cal); 16.4g carbohydrate; 7.1g protein; 7.7g fibre**

- 2 tablespoons olive oil
- 1 medium red onion (170g), cut into thin wedges
- 2 cloves garlic, crushed
- 1 medium eggplant (300g), chopped coarsely
- 1 medium red capsicum (200g), chopped coarsely
- 2 medium zucchini (240g), sliced thickly
- 400g can chickpeas, rinsed, drained
- 4 small egg tomatoes (240g), chopped coarsely
- 2 tablespoons tomato paste
- ½ cup (125ml) water
- ⅔ cup loosely packed fresh basil leaves

1 Heat half the oil in large frying pan; cook onion and garlic, stirring, until onion softens. Remove from pan.
2 Heat remaining oil in same pan; cook eggplant, capsicum and zucchini, stirring, until eggplant is browned lightly.
3 Return onion mixture to pan with chickpeas, tomato, paste and the water; simmer, covered, about 10 minutes or until vegetables soften. Remove from heat; stir in basil.

spicy veal pizzaiola

SPICY VEAL PIZZAIOLA

prep & cook time **30 minutes** serves **4**
nutritional count per serving **14.6g total fat (2.8g saturated fat); 1555kJ (372 cal); 18.8g carbohydrate; 36.3g protein; 4.3g fibre**

2 tablespoons olive oil
2 cloves garlic, crushed
4 slices pancetta (60g), chopped finely
¼ cup (60ml) dry white wine
700g bottled tomato pasta sauce
1 teaspoon dried chilli flakes
4 x 170g veal cutlets
75g baby spinach leaves

1 Heat 2 teaspoons of the oil in large saucepan; cook garlic and pancetta, stirring, 5 minutes. Add wine; cook, stirring, until wine is reduced by half. Add sauce and chilli; simmer, uncovered, about 15 minutes or until sauce thickens.
2 Meanwhile, heat remaining oil in large frying pan. Cook veal until cooked as desired.
3 Remove sauce from heat; stir in spinach. Top veal with sauce.
serve with **375g of cooked pasta of your choice; we used fettuccine.**

CHICKEN, LENTIL AND CAULIFLOWER PILAF

prep & cook time **30 minutes** serves **4**
nutritional count per serving **10.7g total fat (2.3g saturated fat); 1814kJ (434 cal); 50.2g carbohydrate; 36.6g protein; 6.1g fibre**

1 medium brown onion (150g), sliced thinly
1 clove garlic, crushed
2 tablespoons madras curry paste
1 cup (200g) basmati rice
½ small cauliflower (500g), cut into florets
400g can brown lentils, rinsed, drained
1 cup (250ml) chicken stock
1 cup (250ml) water
2 cups (320g) coarsely chopped barbecued chicken (see note)
½ cup firmly packed fresh coriander leaves

1 Cook onion and garlic in heated oiled large frying pan until onion softens. Add paste; cook, stirring, about 5 minutes or until fragrant.
2 Add rice, cauliflower and lentils; stir to coat in onion mixture. Add stock, the water and chicken; bring to the boil. Reduce heat; simmer, covered tightly, about 15 minutes or until rice is tender and liquid has been absorbed. Remove from heat; fluff pilaf with fork. Stir in coriander.
serve with **pappadums and chutney and accompany with lime wedges.**

note **You need half a large barbecued chicken (approximately 500g) to get the amount of shredded meat required for this recipe.**

chicken, lentil and cauliflower pilaf

veal chops with caper sauce

VEAL CHOPS WITH CAPER SAUCE

prep & cook time **30 minutes** serves **6**
nutritional count per serving **10g total fat (3.4g saturated fat); 1346kJ (322 cal); 22.8g carbohydrate; 33g protein; 3.8g fibre**

1kg kipfler potatoes, halved lengthways
1 tablespoon olive oil
6 x 200g veal chops
20g butter
3 cloves garlic, crushed
½ cup (125ml) white grape verjuice
¼ cup (60ml) chicken stock
¼ cup (50g) rinsed, drained baby capers
¼ cup finely chopped fresh flat-leaf parsley
150g baby spinach leaves

1 Boil, steam or microwave potato until tender; drain. Cover to keep warm.
2 Meanwhile, heat oil in large frying pan; cook veal until cooked as desired. Cover veal; stand 5 minutes.
3 Melt butter in same pan; cook garlic, stirring, until fragrant. Add verjuice and stock to pan; bring to the boil, stirring, until thickened slightly. Remove from heat; stir in capers and parsley.
4 Divide spinach and potato among serving plates; top with veal, spoon over sauce.

note **Verjuice is unfermented grape juice with a fresh lemony-vinegar flavour. It's available in supermarkets, usually in the vinegar section.**

chilli con carne

CHILLI CON CARNE

prep & cook time **35 minutes** serves **4**
nutritional count per serving **12.5g total fat (5.2g saturated fat); 1296kJ (310 cal); 16.9g carbohydrate; 24.2g protein; 6.8g fibre**

500g beef mince
2 fresh long red chillies, chopped finely
35g packet taco seasoning mix
400g can diced tomatoes
½ cup (125ml) water
420g can kidney beans, rinsed, drained
⅓ cup coarsely chopped fresh coriander

1 Cook mince in heated oiled large frying pan, stirring, until browned. Add chillies and seasoning mix; cook, stirring, until fragrant.
2 Add undrained tomatoes and the water; bring to the boil. Reduce heat; simmer, uncovered, 15 minutes. Add beans; simmer, uncovered, 5 minutes. Remove from heat, stir in coriander.
serve with **warmed corn tortillas and sour cream.**

pork cutlets with caramelised pear sauce

PORK CUTLETS WITH CARAMELISED PEAR SAUCE

prep & cook time **35 minutes** serves **6**
nutritional count per serving **18.6g total fat (6.6g saturated fat); 1488kJ (356 cal); 18.8g carbohydrate; 22.3g protein; 2.6g fibre**

1 tablespoon olive oil
20g butter
6 x 180g french-trimmed pork cutlets
2 tablespoons brown sugar
3 medium pears (700g), cut crossways into 1.5cm-thick slices
¾ cup (180ml) dry white wine
1 cup (250ml) chicken stock
¼ cup coarsely chopped fresh sage

1 Heat oil and half the butter in large heavy-based frying pan; cook pork, in batches, until cooked as desired. Cover to keep warm.
2 Stir sugar and remaining butter into pan; add pear. Cook about 5 minutes; remove from pan.
3 Add wine to pan; simmer, stirring, 2 minutes. Add stock to pan; simmer, uncovered, about 10 minutes or until liquid has reduced by half. Return pear to pan with sage; simmer until heated through. Serve pork with pear sauce.

note **This is a last-minute recipe; make sure you have any vegetables ready to serve as soon as the pork and pears are ready.**

SNAPPER WITH SPICY TOMATO SAUCE

prep & cook time **30 minutes** serves **4**
nutritional count per serving **12.7g total fat (2.5g saturated fat); 1325kJ (317 cal); 6.3g carbohydrate; 42.5g protein; 2.3g fibre**

2 tablespoons olive oil
3 cloves garlic, crushed
3 shallots (75g), chopped finely
425g can diced tomatoes
1 tablespoon dry sherry
1 tablespoon soy sauce
1 teaspoon sambal oelek
2 teaspoons white sugar
4 snapper fillets (1kg)
75g baby spinach leaves
2 teaspoons red wine vinegar

1 Heat half the oil in small frying pan; cook garlic and shallot, stirring, about 1 minute or until shallot softens. Stir in undrained tomatoes, sherry, sauce, sambal and sugar; bring to the boil. Reduce heat; simmer, uncovered, about 10 minutes or until liquid has reduced by half.
2 Meanwhile, cook fish, uncovered, in heated oiled large frying pan about 10 minutes or until cooked as desired.
3 Place spinach in medium bowl with combined vinegar and remaining oil; toss gently. Serve fish with spicy sauce and spinach salad.

snapper with spicy tomato sauce

BERRY HAZELNUT CRUMBLES

prep + cook time **30 minutes** serves **4**
nutritional count per serving **14.6g total fat (3.2g saturated fat); 915kJ (219 cal); 16.8g carbohydrate; 4.8g protein; 3.9g fibre**

2 cups (300g) frozen mixed berries
1 tablespoon lemon juice
2 tablespoons brown sugar
½ cup (60g) finely chopped roasted hazelnuts
2 tablespoons plain flour
20g cold butter
¼ cup (20g) rolled oats

1 Preheat oven to 220°C/200°C fan-forced. Grease four shallow ¾-cup (180ml) ovenproof dishes; place on oven tray.
2 Combine berries, juice, half the sugar and half the nuts in medium bowl; divide mixture among dishes.
3 Blend or process remaining sugar and nuts with flour and butter until ingredients come together; stir in oats. Sprinkle over berry mixture.
4 Bake, uncovered, about 20 minutes or until browned lightly.
serve with custard or ice-cream.

DESSERTS

peach galette

PEACH GALETTE

prep + cook time **25 minutes** serves **6**
nutritional count per serving **6.4g total fat (0.5g saturated fat); 589kJ (141 cal); 18.2g carbohydrate; 2.1g protein; 1.3g fibre**

1 sheet puff pastry with canola, thawed
3 medium peaches (450g)
1 tablespoon brown sugar
1 tablespoon plum jam, warmed, strained

1 Preheat oven to 220°C/200°C fan-forced. Grease oven tray.
2 Place pastry sheet on tray.
3 Place unpeeled peaches in large heatproof bowl; cover with boiling water. Stand about 1 minute or until skins can be slipped off easily. Slice peaches thinly; discard seeds.
4 Arrange peach slices on pastry, leaving 2cm border around edge; fold over edges of pastry. Sprinkle sugar evenly over peach galette.
5 Bake, uncovered, about 15 minutes or until pastry is browned lightly. Brush hot galette with jam.
serve with **ice-cream.**

note **Dust with a little sifted icing sugar; Any stone fruits, such as plums or nectarines, can be substituted for the peaches.**

CITRUS SALAD WITH LIME AND MINT GRANITA

prep time **15 minutes** serves **4**
nutritional count per serving **0.4g total fat (0g saturated fat); 385kJ (92 cal); 18.1g carbohydrate; 2.1g protein; 2.7g fibre**

2 medium oranges (480g)
2 small pink grapefruits (700g)
⅓ cup finely chopped fresh mint
2 tablespoons icing sugar
1 tablespoon lime juice
2 cups ice cubes

1 Segment orange and grapefruit into medium bowl.
2 Blend or process mint, sugar, juice and ice until ice is crushed; serve with fruit.

citrus salad with lime and mint granita

PINEAPPLE WITH COCONUT

prep time **15 minutes** serves **4**

Peel, core and thinly slice 1 small pineapple. Divide pineapple among four serving dishes; drizzle evenly with ⅓ cup passionfruit pulp and 2 tablespoons Malibu, then sprinkle with ¼ cup toasted flaked coconut.

note **We used Malibu in this recipe, but you can use any coconut-flavoured liqueur you prefer.**

PEARS WITH COFFEE SYRUP

prep & cook time **20 minutes** serves **4**

Peel 4 medium ripe pears; cut in half crossways. Stir ½ cup caster sugar and 2 cups water in medium saucepan over medium heat until sugar dissolves. Add pears; simmer, covered, about 10 minutes or until pears are tender. Remove pears from syrup. Return 1 cup of the syrup to pan; stir in 2 teaspoons instant coffee granules until dissolved. Reassemble pears in serving bowls. Divide the coffee syrup, 4 squares dark eating chocolate and 500ml vanilla ice-cream among serving dishes.

FAST DESSERTS

BALSAMIC STRAWBERRIES

prep time **35 minutes (+ standing)** serves **4**

Combine 500g quartered strawberries with 2 tablespoons balsamic vinegar and ⅓ cup icing sugar in medium bowl; stand 25 minutes. Divide strawberry mixture among serving dishes, top evenly with ⅓ cup crème fraîche.

note **Strawberries can also be served with yogurt or light sour cream.**

MANGO AND WHITE CHOCOLATE ROCKY ROAD CREAMS

prep time **15 minutes** serves **4**

Coarsely chop 2 medium mangoes. Blend or process half the mango until smooth. Transfer to medium bowl; fold in 1 cup greek-style yogurt. Beat ½ cup thickened cream and 2 teaspoons caster sugar in small bowl with electric mixer until firm peaks form; fold into mango mixture. Divide half the chopped mango among four serving glasses; top with half the cream mixture, then 250g packet chopped white chocolate rocky road, remaining cream mixture and remaining chopped mango.

rhubarb soufflé

RHUBARB SOUFFLÉ

prep & cook time **30 minutes** serves **4**
nutritional count per serving **1.1g total fat (0.1g saturated fat); 635kJ (152 cal); 31g carbohydrate; 3.3g protein; 1.3g fibre**

cooking-oil spray
½ cup (110g) caster sugar
1½ cups (165g) coarsely chopped rhubarb
1 tablespoon water
3 egg whites
1 tablespoon icing sugar

1 Preheat oven to 200°C/180°C fan-forced.
2 Spray inside of four 1-cup (250ml) ovenproof dishes with cooking-oil spray. Sprinkle base and sides of dishes with 2 tablespoons of the caster sugar. Stand dishes on oven tray.
3 Combine rhubarb, the water and 2 tablespoons of the caster sugar in small saucepan. Cook, stirring, over medium heat, about 10 minutes or until mixture thickens. Transfer mixture to medium heatproof bowl.
4 Meanwhile, beat egg whites in small bowl with electric mixer until soft peaks form. Gradually add remaining caster sugar; beat until firm peaks form.
5 Fold egg-white mixture into warm rhubarb mixture, in two batches. Spoon mixture into dishes. Bake in oven about 12 minutes.
6 Serve soufflés immediately, dusted with sifted icing sugar.

CHOCOLATE FUDGE CAKES WITH COFFEE SYRUP

prep & cook time **35 minutes** makes **12**
nutritional count per cake **5.1g total fat (2g saturated fat); 895kJ (214 cal); 39.5g carbohydrate; 4.2g protein; 1.2g fibre**

½ cup (50g) cocoa powder
1 cup (220g) firmly packed brown sugar
½ cup (125ml) boiling water
85g dark cooking chocolate, chopped finely
2 egg yolks
¼ cup (30g) almond meal
⅓ cup (50g) wholemeal plain flour
4 egg whites

coffee syrup
¾ cup (165g) firmly packed brown sugar
¾ cup (180ml) water
1 tablespoon instant coffee powder

1 Preheat oven to 160°C/140°C fan-forced. Lightly grease 12-hole (⅓-cup/80ml) muffin pan.
2 Combine sifted cocoa and sugar in large bowl; blend in the water then chocolate, stir until smooth. Stir in egg yolks, almond meal and flour.
3 Beat egg whites in small bowl with electric mixer until soft peaks form. Fold egg whites into chocolate mixture, in two batches; divide mixture among pan holes. Bake, uncovered, about 20 minutes.
4 Meanwhile, make coffee syrup.
5 Stand cakes in pan 5 minutes, divide among plates; drizzle hot cakes with hot coffee syrup.
coffee syrup Stir sugar and the water in small saucepan over low heat until sugar dissolves; bring to the boil. Reduce heat; simmer, uncovered, without stirring, about 15 minutes or until syrup thickens. Stir in coffee; strain into small heatproof jug.

chocolate fudge cakes with coffee syrup

APRICOTS WITH SPICED RICOTTA

prep & cook time **25 minutes** serves **4**
nutritional count per serving **2.9g total fat (1.4g saturated fat); 568kJ (136 cal); 22g carbohydrate; 4.1g protein; 2.2g fibre**

4 large fresh apricots (220g), halved, stones removed
½ cup (45g) rolled oats
2 tablespoons finely chopped dried apricots
1 tablespoon brown sugar
1 tablespoon honey
1 tablespoon warm water
⅓ cup (80g) smooth reduced-fat ricotta cheese
¼ teaspoon ground cinnamon
pinch ground cardamom

1 Preheat oven to 200°C/180°C fan-forced.
2 Place fresh apricots, cut-side up, on oven tray; sprinkle with combined oats, dried apricots, sugar, honey and the water. Bake about 15 minutes or until fruit is tender.
3 Meanwhile, combine cheese and spices in small bowl. Serve fruit with spiced ricotta.

summer berry stack

SUMMER BERRY STACK

prep & cook time **25 minutes** serves **4**
nutritional count per serving **7.2g total fat (3g saturated fat) 1313kJ (314 cal) 55.3g carbohydrate 7.5g protein 9.7g fibre**

450g brioche loaf
250g strawberries, sliced thickly
150g raspberries
150g blueberries
1 tablespoon icing sugar
blackberry coulis
300g frozen blackberries
¼ cup (40g) icing sugar
¼ cup (60ml) water

1 Make blackberry coulis.
2 Cut 12 x 1cm-thick slices from brioche loaf. Using 7cm cutter, cut one round from each slice.
3 Combine berries in medium bowl.
4 Place one bread round on each of four serving plates; divide a third of the berries among rounds. Place another round on top of each stack; divide half of the remaining berries among stacks. Place remaining rounds on berry stacks; top with remaining berries.
5 Pour coulis over stacks; dust each with sifted icing sugar.
blackberry coulis Stir ingredients in medium saucepan over high heat; bring to the boil. Reduce heat; simmer, uncovered, 3 minutes. Strain coulis into medium jug; cool 10 minutes.

tip **Toast any leftover brioche loaf for breakfast, or use it to make a bread and butter pudding.**

BERRY, COCONUT AND YOGURT PARFAITS

prep time **10 minutes** serves **6**
nutritional count per serving **5.2g total fat (3.3g saturated fat); 882kJ (211 cal); 31.5g carbohydrate; 6.5g protein; 1.1g fibre**

1 cup (150g) frozen mixed berries
1 tablespoon caster sugar
1 tablespoon coconut-flavoured liqueur
1 cup (250ml) raspberry and cranberry juice
12 sponge-finger biscuits (140g)

berry, coconut and yogurt parfaits

500g vanilla yogurt
2 tablespoons flaked coconut, toasted

1 Blend or process berries, sugar, liqueur and ¼ cup of juice until smooth.
2 Dip biscuits in remaining juice; divide among six 1½-cup (375ml) serving glasses.
3 Divide half the yogurt among glasses; top with half the berry mixture. Repeat layering with remaining yogurt and berry mixture. Sprinkle with coconut.

note **This dessert can be made several hours in advance; store, covered, in the refrigerator.**

ASIAN GREENS, BABY a packaged mix of baby buk choy, choy sum, gai lan and water spinach. It is available from Asian food stores and selected supermarkets.

BABA GHANOUSH roasted eggplant dip or spread.

BEEF

eye fillet steaks also known as beef tenderloin or fillet.

new-york cut steaks boneless striploin steak.

BEETROOT also known as red beets or beets; firm, round root vegetable.

BREADS

brioche rich, french bread made with yeast, butter and eggs. Available from pâtisseries or better bakeries.

ciabatta in Italian, the word means slipper, which is the traditional shape of this popular white bread with a crisp crust. Also available as rolls.

lavash flat, unleavened bread of Mediterranean origin.

turkish also known as pide; comes in long (about 45cm) flat loaves as well as individual rounds.

breadcrumbs, stale one- or two-day-old bread made into crumbs by blending or processing.

BROCCOLINI a cross between broccoli and chinese kale; milder and sweeter than broccoli. Each long stem is topped by a loose floret that closely resembles broccoli; from floret to stem, broccolini is completely edible.

BUK CHOY, BABY also known as pak kat farang or shanghai bok choy; is much smaller and more tender than more mature buk choy. Most commonly used of all Asian greens.

BUTTER use salted or unsalted (sweet) butter; 125g is equal to one stick (4 ounces) of butter.

CAPSICUM also known as bell pepper or, simply, pepper.

CHICKPEAS also called garbanzos, hummus or channa; an irregularly round, sandy-coloured legume.

CHINESE COOKING WINE also known as hao hsing or chinese rice wine; made from fermented rice, wheat, sugar and salt. Found in Asian food shops; if you can't find it, replace with mirin or sherry.

CHOY SUM also known as pakaukeo or flowering cabbage, a member of the buk choy family; easy to identify with its long stems, light green leaves and yellow flowers. Is eaten stems and all.

CORIANDER also known as pak chee, cilantro or chinese parsley; bright-green leafy herb with a pungent flavour. Both the stems and roots are used; wash well before using. Also available ground or as seeds; do not substitute for fresh coriander as the tastes are different.

CUCUMBER

lebanese short, slender and thin-skinned. Probably the most popular variety because of its tender, edible skin, tiny, yielding seeds, and sweet, fresh and flavoursome taste.

telegraph long and green with ridges running down its entire length; also known as continental cucumber.

EGGPLANT also known as aubergine.

FIVE-SPICE POWDER (chinese five-spice) a fragrant mixture of ground cinnamon, cloves, star anise, sichuan pepper and fennel seeds.

FLOUR, PLAIN an all-purpose flour made from wheat.

GAI LAN also known as chinese broccoli, gai larn, kanah, gai lum and chinese kale; appreciated more for its stems than its coarse leaves.

HAZELNUTS also known as filberts.

KAFFIR LIME LEAVES aromatic leaves of a citrus tree; used similarly to bay leaves. A strip of fresh lime peel may be substituted for each kaffir lime leaf.

KIPFLER POTATOES small, finger-shaped potato having a nutty flavour.

LEMON GRASS a tall, clumping, lemon-smelling and -tasting, sharp-edged grass; the white lower part is chopped and used in cooking.

MARINARA MIX a mix of uncooked, chopped seafood available from fish markets and fishmongers.

MINCE also known as ground meat.

MIRIN is a Japanese champagne-coloured cooking wine; made of glutinous rice and alcohol and used expressly for cooking. Should not be confused with sake.

NOODLES

hokkien also known as stir-fry noodles; fresh wheat noodles resembling thick, yellow-brown spaghetti needing no pre-cooking before being used.

fresh rice also known as ho fun, khao pun, sen yau, pho or kway tiau, depending on the country of manufacture. Can be purchased in strands of various widths or large sheets weighing about 500g, which are to be cut into the desired noodle size. Chewy and pure white, they do not need pre-cooking before use.

ONIONS

green also known as scallion or, incorrectly, shallot; an immature onion picked before the bulb has formed, having a long, bright-green edible stalk.

red also known as spanish, red spanish or bermuda onion; a sweet-flavoured, large, purple-red onion.

GLOSSARY

PARSLEY, FLAT-LEAF also known as continental or italian parsley.

PRESERVED LEMON RIND a North African specialty; quartered lemons are preserved in salt and lemon juice. To use, remove and discard pulp, squeeze juice from rind, rinse rind well; slice thinly. Sold in jars or singly by delicatessens and major supermarkets; once opened, store under refrigeration.

ROCKET also known as arugula, rugula and rucola; a peppery-tasting green leaf used similarly to baby spinach leaves. Baby rocket leaves are both smaller and less peppery.

ROLLED OATS oat groats (husked oats) steamed-softened, flattened with rollers, dried and packaged for consumption as a cereal product.

SAMBAL OELEK (also ulek or olek) a salty paste made from ground chillies and vinegar.

SAUCES

char siu a chinese barbecue sauce made from sugar, water, salt, honey, fermented soybean paste, soy sauce, malt syrup and spices. It can be found in most supermarkets.

hoisin a thick, sweet and spicy paste made from salted fermented soya beans, onions and garlic.

oyster Asian in origin, this rich, brown sauce is made from oysters and their brine, cooked with salt and soy sauce, and thickened with starches.

soy *japanese soy* is an all-purpose low-sodium soy sauce; possibly the best table soy and the one to choose if you only want one variety. *light soy* is fairly thin in consistency and, while paler than the others, is the saltiest tasting; used in dishes in which the natural colour of the ingredients is to be maintained. *kecap manis* also known as ketjap manis; a thick soy sauce with added sugar and spices.

sweet chilli a comparatively mild, Thai-type sauce made from red chillies, sugar, garlic and vinegar.

worcestershire a dark coloured condiment made from garlic, soy sauce, tamarind, onions, molasses, lime, anchovies and vinegar.

SPINACH also known as english spinach and, incorrectly, silver beet.

STAR ANISE a dried star-shaped fruit of a tree native to China. The pods have an astringent aniseed or licorice flavour. Available whole and ground.

SPONGE-FINGER BISCUITS also known as savoiardi, savoy biscuits, lady's fingers or sponge fingers; they are Italian-style crisp fingers made from sponge cake mixture.

SUGAR

caster also known as superfine or finely granulated table sugar.

icing also known as confectioners' or powdered sugar; granulated sugar crushed with added cornflour.

palm also known as nam tan pip, jaggery, jawa or gula melaka; made from the sap of the sugar palm tree. Light brown to black in colour and usually sold in rock-hard cakes. It can be substituted with brown sugar, if unavailable.

white a coarse, granulated table sugar, also known as crystal sugar.

SUGAR SNAP PEAS also known as honey snap peas; fresh small peas that can be eaten whole, pod and all, similarly to snow peas.

SUMAC a purple-red, astringent spice; adds a tart, lemony flavour. Available from major supermarkets and speciality spice stores.

TACO SEASONING MIX a packaged seasoning meant to duplicate the Mexican sauce made from oregano, cumin, chillies and other spices.

THAI BASIL has smallish leaves and a sweet licorice/aniseed taste; is available from Asian supermarkets and greengrocers.

THAI CHILLI JAM a combination of garlic, shallots, chilli, tomato paste, fish sauce, galangal, spices and shrimp paste. It is sold under various names, and can be found in the Asian food section of supermarkets.

VEAL SCHNITZELS thinly sliced steak available crumbed or plain (uncrumbed); we use plain schnitzel, sometimes called escalopes.

VINEGAR

balsamic originally from Modena, Italy, there are now many balsamic vinegars on the market ranging in pungency and quality depending on how, and how long, they have been aged. Quality can be determined up to a point by price; use the most expensive sparingly. It is a deep rich brown colour with a sweet and sour flavour. Available from supermarkets.

raspberry made from raspberries steeped in a white wine vinegar.

red wine based on red wine.

white based on spirit of cane sugar.

white wine made from a blend of white wines.

WOMBOK also known as peking or chinese cabbage, or petsai. Elongated in shape with pale green, crinkly leaves; is the most common cabbage used in South-East Asia.

ZUCCHINI also known as courgette; small, pale- or dark-green, yellow or white vegetable belonging to the squash family.

CONVERSION CHART

MEASURES

One Australian metric measuring cup holds approximately 250ml, one Australian metric tablespoon holds 20ml, one Australian metric teaspoon holds 5ml.

The difference between one country's measuring cups and another's is within a 2- or 3-teaspoon variance, and will not affect your cooking results. North America, New Zealand and the United Kingdom use a 15ml tablespoon. All cup and spoon measurements are level. The most accurate way of measuring dry ingredients is to weigh them. When measuring liquids, use a clear glass or plastic jug with metric markings.

We use large eggs with an average weight of 60g.

DRY MEASURES

METRIC	IMPERIAL
15g	½oz
30g	1oz
60g	2oz
90g	3oz
125g	4oz (¼lb)
155g	5oz
185g	6oz
220g	7oz
250g	8oz (½lb)
280g	9oz
315g	10oz
345g	11oz
375g	12oz (¾lb)
410g	13oz
440g	14oz
470g	15oz
500g	16oz (1lb)
750g	24oz (1½lb)
1kg	32oz (2lb)

OVEN TEMPERATURES

These oven temperatures are only a guide for conventional ovens. For fan-forced ovens, check the manufacturer's manual.

	°C (CELSIUS)	°F (FAHRENHEIT)	GAS MARK
Very slow	120	250	½
Slow	150	275-300	1-2
Moderately slow	160	325	3
Moderate	180	350-375	4-5
Moderately hot	200	400	6
Hot	220	425-450	7-8
Very hot	240	475	9

LIQUID MEASURES

METRIC	IMPERIAL
30ml	1 fluid oz
60ml	2 fluid oz
100ml	3 fluid oz
125ml	4 fluid oz
150ml	5 fluid oz (¼ pint/1 gill)
190ml	6 fluid oz
250ml	8 fluid oz
300ml	10 fluid oz (½ pint)
500ml	16 fluid oz
600ml	20 fluid oz (1 pint)
1000ml (1 litre)	1¾ pints

LENGTH MEASURES

METRIC	IMPERIAL
3mm	⅛in
6mm	¼in
1cm	½in
2cm	¾in
2.5cm	1in
5cm	2in
6cm	2½in
8cm	3in
10cm	4in
13cm	5in
15cm	6in
18cm	7in
20cm	8in
23cm	9in
25cm	10in
28cm	11in
30cm	12in (1ft)

INDEX

ACP BOOKS
General manager Christine Whiston
Editor-in-chief Susan Tomnay
Creative director Hieu Chi Nguyen
Art director & designer Hannah Blackmore
Senior editor Wendy Bryant
Food director Pamela Clark
Nutritional information Rebecca Squadrito
Sales & rights director Brian Cearnes
Marketing manager Bridget Cody
Senior business analyst Rebecca Varela
Circulation manager Jarna Mclean
Operations manager David Scotto
Production manager Victoria Jefferys

ACP Books are published by ACP Magazines
a division of PBL Media Pty Limited
PBL Media, Chief Executive officer Ian Law
Publishing & sales director, Women's lifestyle Lynette Phillips
Editor-at-large, Women's lifestyle Pat Ingram
Marketing director, Women's lifestyle Matthew Dominello
Commercial manager, Women's lifestyle Seymour Cohen
Research Director, Women's lifestyle Justin Stone

Produced by ACP Books, Sydney.

Published by ACP Books, a division of ACP Magazines Ltd, 54 Park St, Sydney; GPO Box 4088, Sydney, NSW 2001.
phone (02) 9282 8618; fax (02) 9267 9438. acpbooks@acpmagazines.com.au; www.acpbooks.com.au

Printed by Toppan Printing Co., China.

Australia Distributed by Network Services, phone +61 2 9282 8777;
fax +61 2 9264 3278; networkweb@networkservicescompany.com.au
United Kingdom Distributed by Australian Consolidated Press (UK), phone (01604) 642 200;
fax (01604) 642 300; books@acpuk.com
New Zealand Distributed by Netlink Distribution Company, phone (9) 366 9966; ask@ndc.co.nz
South Africa Distributed by PSD Promotions, phone (27 11) 392 6065/6/7;
fax (27 11) 392 6079/80; orders@psdprom.co.za
Canada Distributed by Publishers Group Canada
phone (800) 663 5714; fax (800) 565 3770; service@raincoast.com

After work healthy / food director Pamela Clark.
ISBN: 978186396 8553 (pbk.)
Notes: Includes index.
Subjects: Cookery (Natural foods)
Quick and easy cookery.
Other Authors/Contributors: Clark, Pamela.
Dewey Number: 641.5637

Cover Veal chops with caper sauce, page 61
Photographer Ian Wallace
Stylist Louise Pickford
Food preparation Nicole Jennings

To order books, phone 136 116 (within Australia) or order online at www.acpbooks.com.au
Send recipe enquiries to: recipeenquiries@acpmagazines.com.au